infinity

Schiffer **Kids**®

4880 Lower Valley Road, Atglen, PA 19310

THE CYCLE OF WATER

WATER TRANSFORMS INTO ICE AND STEAM
WITH COLD AND HEAT, HOW MAGIC THEY SEEM.

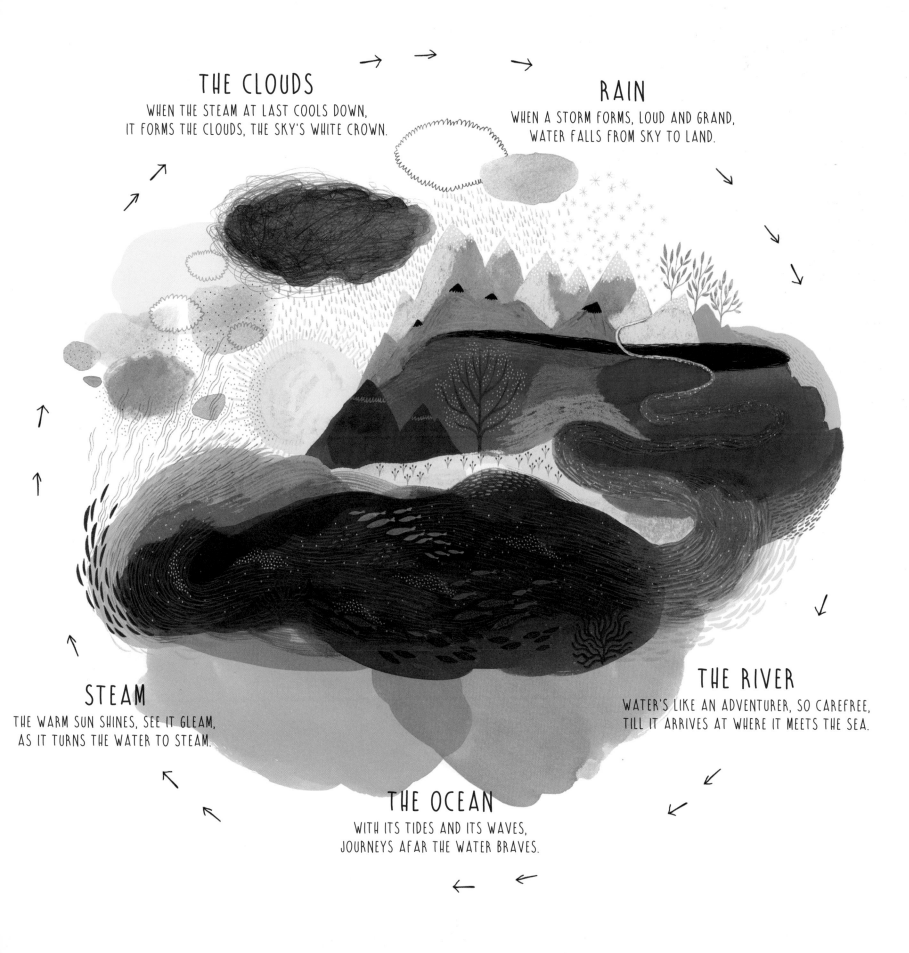

THE CLOUDS

WHEN THE STEAM AT LAST COOLS DOWN,
IT FORMS THE CLOUDS, THE SKY'S WHITE CROWN.

RAIN

WHEN A STORM FORMS, LOUD AND GRAND,
WATER FALLS FROM SKY TO LAND.

THE RIVER

WATER'S LIKE AN ADVENTURER, SO CAREFREE,
TILL IT ARRIVES AT WHERE IT MEETS THE SEA.

STEAM

THE WARM SUN SHINES, SEE IT GLEAM,
AS IT TURNS THE WATER TO STEAM.

THE OCEAN

WITH ITS TIDES AND ITS WAVES,
JOURNEYS AFAR THE WATER BRAVES.

JUST BECAUSE WE STOP SEEING A DROP OF WATER
DOESN'T MEAN THAT IT DISAPPEARS.
IT JUST BECOMES SOMETHING ELSE,
SOMETHING NEW OUR EYES CAN'T SEE
AND OUR MINDS CAN'T COMPREHEND.

WE FORGET THAT THE WATER CYCLE
AND THE LIFE CYCLE ARE ONE.

—JACQUES-YVES COUSTEAU
FRENCH RESEARCHER AND EXPLORER

THE LIFE CYCLE OF BUTTERFLIES

THE BUTTERFLY IS THE MULTICOLORED STAR
OF A BEAUTIFUL PERFORMANCE, UNMATCHED SO FAR.

THE EGG
ON A LEAF, GREEN AND TENDER,
THE BUTTERFLY PLACES ITS FUTURE SPLENDOR.

THE CATERPILLAR
FROM THE EGG THE CATERPILLAR EMERGES
TO TRY TO SOOTHE ITS HUNGER URGES.

THE BUTTERFLY
WHEN A DELICATE BUTTERFLY IS BORN,
COLORS DO ITS WINGS ADORN.

THE CHRYSALIS
THE CATERPILLAR WRAPS ITSELF UP TIGHT;
'TIS THE HOUR FOR THE MAGIC TO IGNITE.

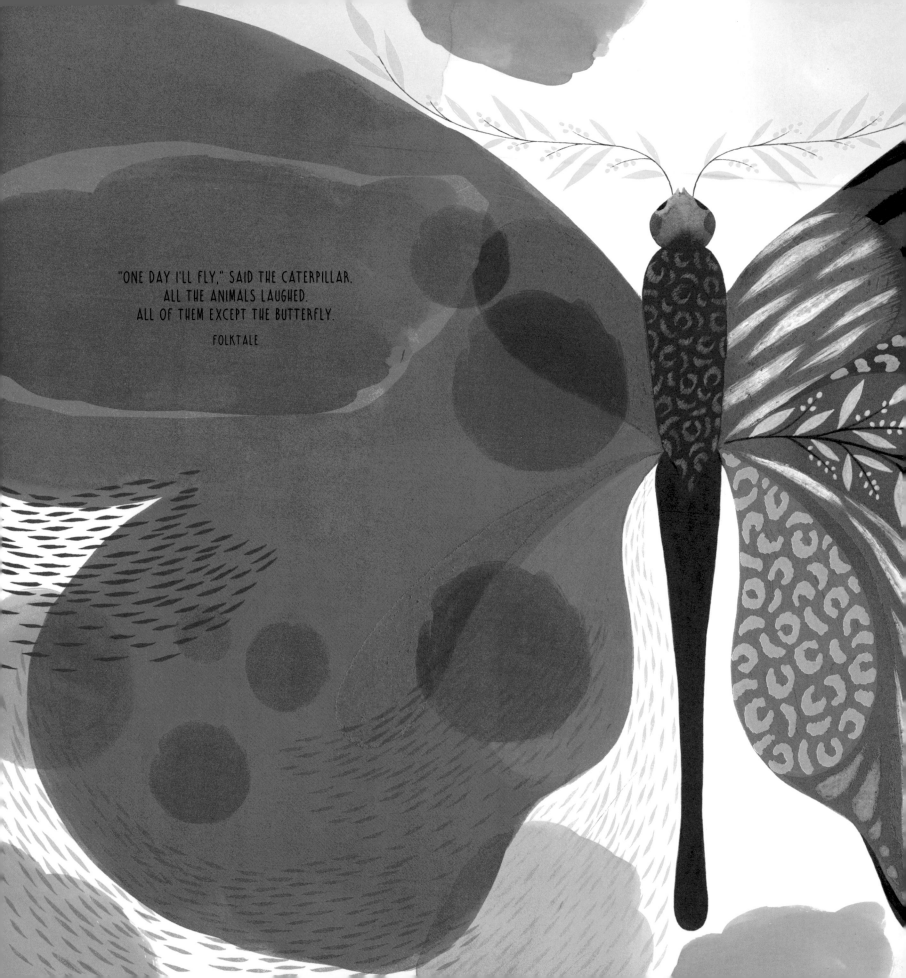

"ONE DAY I'LL FLY," SAID THE CATERPILLAR.
ALL THE ANIMALS LAUGHED.
ALL OF THEM EXCEPT THE BUTTERFLY.

FOLKTALE

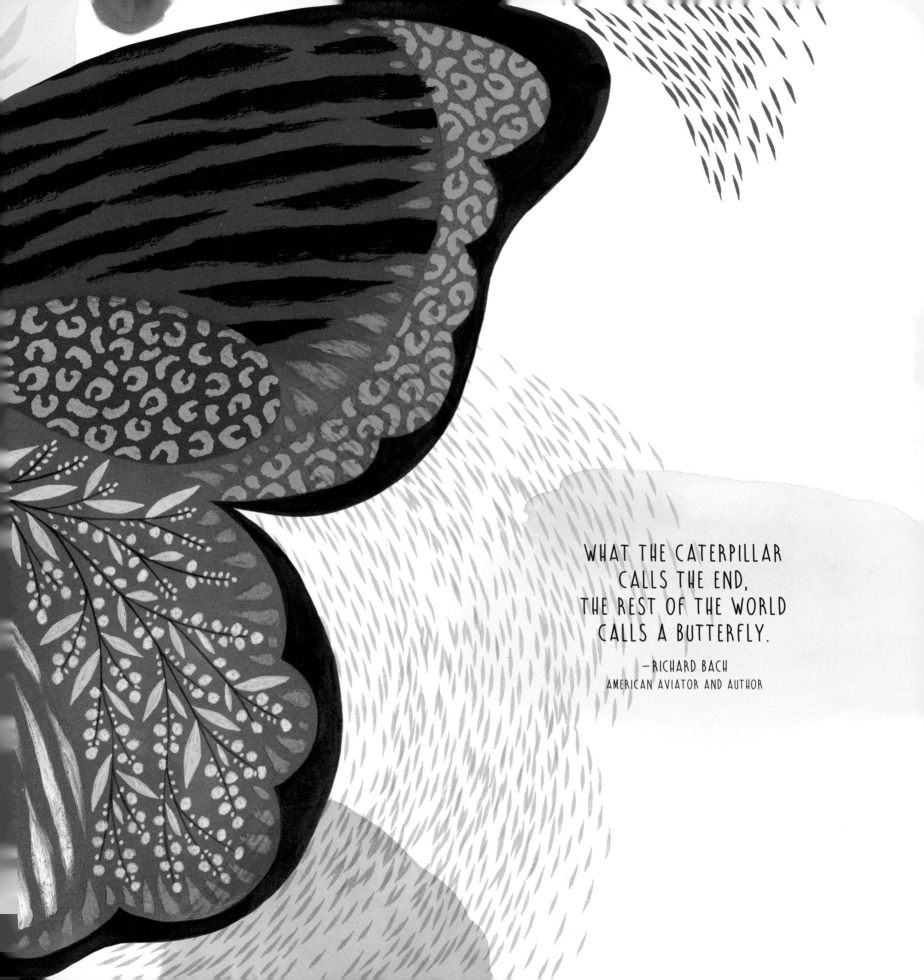

WHAT THE CATERPILLAR
CALLS THE END,
THE REST OF THE WORLD
CALLS A BUTTERFLY.

–RICHARD BACH
AMERICAN AVIATOR AND AUTHOR

THE LIFE CYCLE OF STORKS

STORK COUPLES MATE FOR LIFE,
CHANGING PARTNERS ONLY IF ONE OF THEM DIES.

THE STORK COUPLE
THEY PROMISE LOVE ETERNAL, SIDE BY SIDE,
TRAVELING TOGETHER FAR AND WIDE.

THE NEST
THE NESTS ARE BUILT WAY UP HIGH,
TO PROTECT THE EGGS THERE IN THE SKY.

THE YOUNG STORKS
THE TIME HAS COME TO GO AND FLY.
IN SEARCH OF LOVE AND FREEDOM,
THEY SAY GOODBYE.

THE CHICKS
THE CHICKS PEEP AND MAKE LITTLE LEAPS.
MOM AND DAD BRING FOOD IN THEIR BEAKS!

TO LOVE IS ACCEPTING,
WITH YOUR HEART WIDE OPEN,
ALL SOMEONE'S GREATNESS
AND ALL THEIR WEAKNESS.

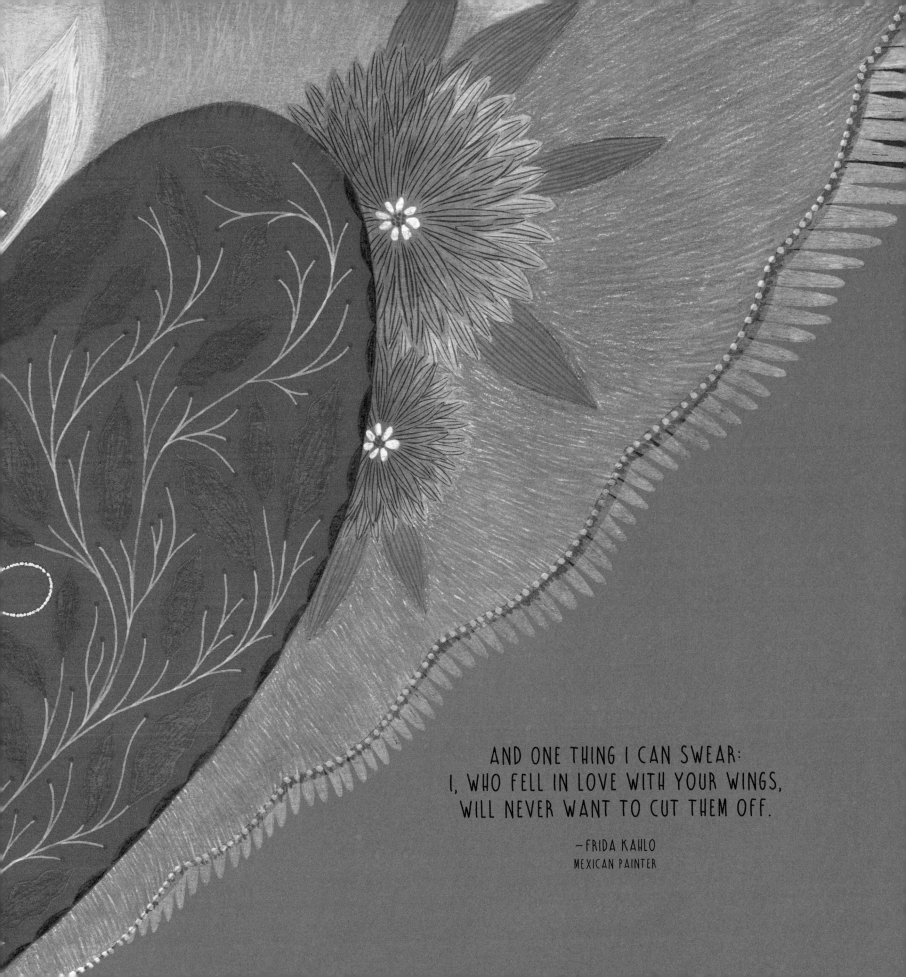

AND ONE THING I CAN SWEAR:
I, WHO FELL IN LOVE WITH YOUR WINGS,
WILL NEVER WANT TO CUT THEM OFF.

—FRIDA KAHLO
MEXICAN PAINTER

THE CYCLE OF THE SEASONS OF A YEAR

THE EARTH'S WONDERFUL JOURNEY AROUND THE SUN GIVES RISE TO THE CHANGING SEASONS.

WINTER
WITH THE ARRIVAL OF OLD MAN WINTER
COME THE COLD AND WINDS SO BITTER.

SPRING
IN FIELDS, FLOWERS SHOW
THEIR COLORFUL FACES.
THE ANIMALS COME OUT OF
THEIR HIDING PLACES.

FALL
THE SUMMER'S BRILLIANT COLOR SHOW
IS NOW THE FALL'S YELLOWS
AND GOLDS AGLOW.

SUMMER
AS WATERMELONS AND CHERRIES RIPEN
IN THE SUMMER SUN,
FAMILIES VACATION, PICNIC,
AND PLAY GAMES OUTSIDE FOR FUN.

THE CREATION OF SOMETHING NEW
MEANS SOMETHING OLD MUST BE THROUGH.
IT'S ALL PART OF A MAGIC WHEEL THAT TURNS.
IT NEVER STOPS—EACH PHASE RETURNS.

THE TREES MEDITATE IN WINTER,
THANKS TO THIS, THEY FLOWER IN THE SPRING,
THEN GIVE SHADE AND FRUIT IN THE SUMMER,
AND RID THEMSELVES OF THE EXTRANEOUS IN THE FALL.

—ZEN POEM
BUDDHIST SCHOOL OF THOUGHT

THE CYCLE OF THE MIGRATING BIRDS

A GREAT JOURNEY THROUGH THE SKIES OF THE WORLD,
SEARCHING FOR SPRING AND LEAVES UNFURLED.

THE LANDS OF THE NORTH
THE NORTH IS RICH IN WATER AND FOOD,
AN IDEAL PLACE TO FEED THEIR BROOD.

JOURNEY
TO THE SOUTH
WHEN IN THE NORTH THE COLD WINDS BLOW,
THEY SEEK THE WARMTH IN THE SOUTH BELOW.

JOURNEY TO THE NORTH
WHEN THE NORTH CHANGES ITS SEASON,
THE INTREPID BIRDS TAKE WING FOR A REASON.

THE LANDS OF THE SOUTH
AFTER A LONG AND VERY HARD FLIGHT,
THEY REACH THE WARMTH WITH MUCH DELIGHT.

SINCE TIME IMMORTAL,
ANIMALS AND HUMANS
HAVE CROSSED MOUNTAINS AND SEAS
IN SEARCH OF NEW OPPORTUNITIES.
THE PLANET IS EVERYONE'S HOME.
THERE SHOULD BE NO BORDERS THAT DIVIDE US,
ONLY BRIDGES THAT BRING US CLOSER TOGETHER.

SEE THE WORLD.
IT'S MORE FANTASTIC THAN ANY DREAM.

—RAY BRADBURY
AMERICAN WRITER

THE LIFE CYCLE OF FISH

SWIMMING AROUND ON THE OCEAN FLOOR
ARE THE OLDEST ANIMALS ON PLANET EARTH.

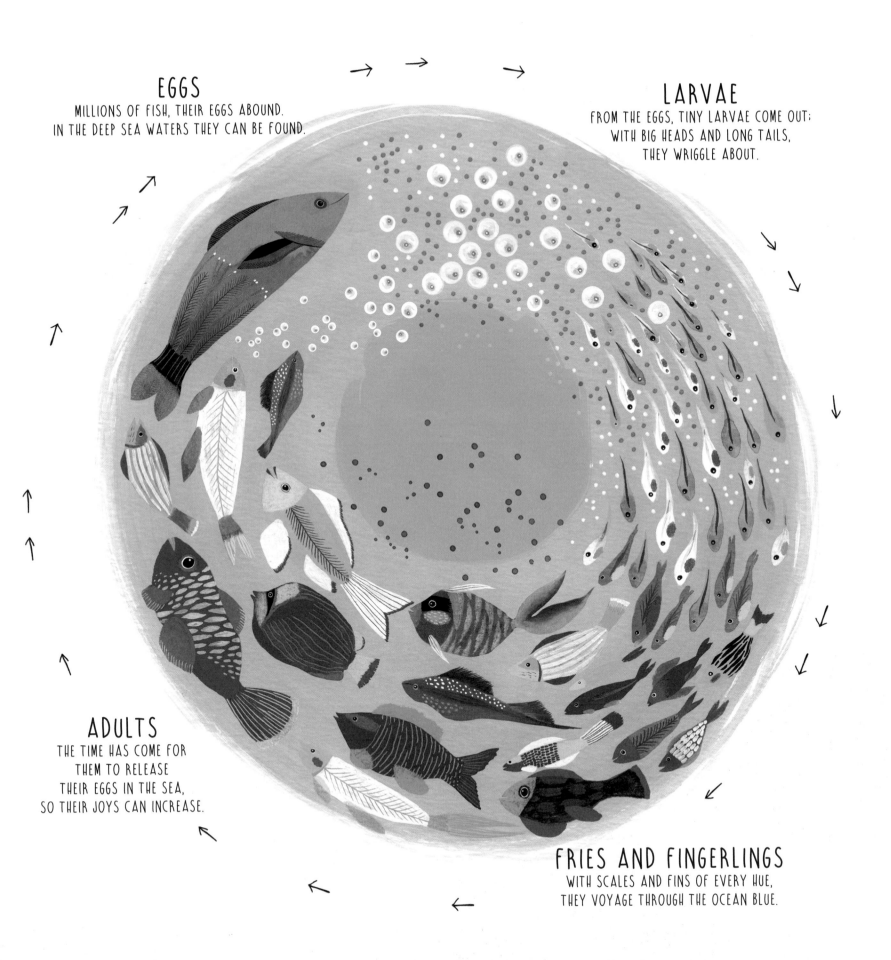

EGGS
MILLIONS OF FISH, THEIR EGGS ABOUND.
IN THE DEEP SEA WATERS THEY CAN BE FOUND.

LARVAE
FROM THE EGGS, TINY LARVAE COME OUT;
WITH BIG HEADS AND LONG TAILS,
THEY WRIGGLE ABOUT.

ADULTS
THE TIME HAS COME FOR
THEM TO RELEASE
THEIR EGGS IN THE SEA,
SO THEIR JOYS CAN INCREASE.

FRIES AND FINGERLINGS
WITH SCALES AND FINS OF EVERY HUE,
THEY VOYAGE THROUGH THE OCEAN BLUE.

LIFE TRACES ITS ORIGINS TO THE WATER.
THROUGH THE EVOLUTION OF SPECIES;
THE HUMAN BEING CAME ABOUT FROM THE LAND ANIMALS.
I IMAGINE THAT WITH A CERTAIN NOSTALGIA ABOUT WHAT WE WERE,
WE ARE STILL IN LOVE WITH THE INFINITE BEAUTY
AND GRANDIOSITY OF WHAT WAS ONCE
OUR HOME: THE OCEAN.

THE SEA IS EVERYTHING.
IT COVERS SEVEN-TENTHS OF THE TERRESTRIAL GLOBE.
ITS BREATH IS PURE AND HEALTHY.
IT IS AN IMMENSE DESERT,
WHERE MAN IS NEVER LONELY,
FOR HE FEELS LIFE STIRRING ON ALL SIDES.

—JULES VERNE
FRENCH NOVELIST

THE LIFE CYCLE OF CHICKENS

WHAT CAME FIRST,
THE CHICKEN OR THE EGG?

THE EGG
IN THE HENHOUSE, AMONG THE HAY,
A DELICATE EGG DOES SOFTLY LAY.

THE HEN
THE HEN'S FEATHERS ARE QUITE A DISPLAY.
SHE LAYS AN EGG EVERY DAY.

THE CHICK
THE LITTLE YELLOW CHICKS BREAK THE EGGSHELL;
"PEEP, PEEP, PEEP!" MOM HEARS THEM YELL.

THE THEORY OF THE EVOLUTION OF THE SPECIES
AFFIRMS THAT THE EGG CAME BEFORE THE CHICKEN.
ON PLANET EARTH, EGGS EXISTED
MANY, MANY YEARS BEFORE CHICKENS DID.

IT IS NOT THE STRONGEST OF THE SPECIES
THAT SURVIVES, NOR THE MOST INTELLIGENT,
IT IS THE ONE THAT IS MOST ADAPTABLE TO CHANGE.

— AN INTERPRETATION OF THE THEORIES OF CHARLES DARWIN
ENGLISH NATURALIST

THE PHASES OF THE MOON

IN A COSMIC PROMISE TO THE EARTH,
THE MOON ORBITS AROUND WHAT GAVE IT BIRTH.

NEW MOON
TONIGHT, THE MOON HIDES AWAY.
DARKNESS FALLS ACROSS THE BAY.

WAXING MOON
NOW THE MOON PEEKS
OUT WITH CARE,
A GOLDEN HORN CURVING
IN THE NIGHT AIR.

WANING MOON
THIS MOON BECOMES MORE
AND MORE SLENDER;
LITTLE BY LITTLE IT
LOSES ITS SPLENDOR.

FULL MOON
THE MOON IS SHINING BRIGHT AND ROUND,
ITS BEAUTY ALWAYS READY TO ASTOUND.

ONE NIGHT I OBSERVED
THE MOON AT LENGTH.
I MANAGED TO PERCEIVE HOW
THE SUN ILLUMINATES ITS EDGES.
IT WAS THEN THAT THE SKY WAS NO LONGER FLAT
AND THE UNIVERSE OPENED ABOVE MY HEAD,
DEEP, INFINITE, AND MAGICAL.

LOOK DEEP INTO
NATURE AND YOU WILL
UNDERSTAND EVERYTHING BETTER.

— ALBERT EINSTEIN
GERMAN SCIENTIST

THE FOOD CHAIN

A MAGICAL WHEEL THAT FEEDS
THE PLANTS AND ANIMALS HERE ON EARTH.

THE SQUIRREL
(PRIMARY CONSUMER)
THESE FURRY FRIENDS EAT THE ALMONDS SO SWEET
THAT SUMMER PROVIDES WITH BRANCHES REPLETE.

THE EAGLE
(SECONDARY CONSUMER)
THE LITTLE SQUIRREL IS DEVOURED
BY A HUNGRY EAGLE THAT NATURE EMPOWERED.

THE ALMOND TREE
(PRODUCER)
ITS ROOTS EXTEND DOWN INTO THE GROUND,
SEEKING WATER AND NUTRIENTS, FEELING AROUND.

DECOMPOSING THINGS
THEY ARE THE HEROES OF THE MAGIC WHEEL,
BREAKING THINGS DOWN, GIVING THE SOIL A MEAL.

NATURE IS WISE.
IT TAKES ONLY WHAT IT NEEDS,
AND GIVES BACK WHAT IT NO LONGER USES.

OF ALL ANIMALS IN GOD'S CREATION,
MAN IS THE ONLY ONE
WHO DRINKS WITHOUT BEING THIRSTY,
EATS WITHOUT BEING HUNGRY,
AND TALKS WITHOUT HAVING SOMETHING TO SAY.

—JOHN STEINBECK
AMERICAN WRITER

THE CYCLE OF DAY AND NIGHT

THE SUN ILLUMINATES ONE PART OF THE EARTH,
AND EVERYTHING RESTS IN THE NIGHT ON THE OPPOSITE SIDE.

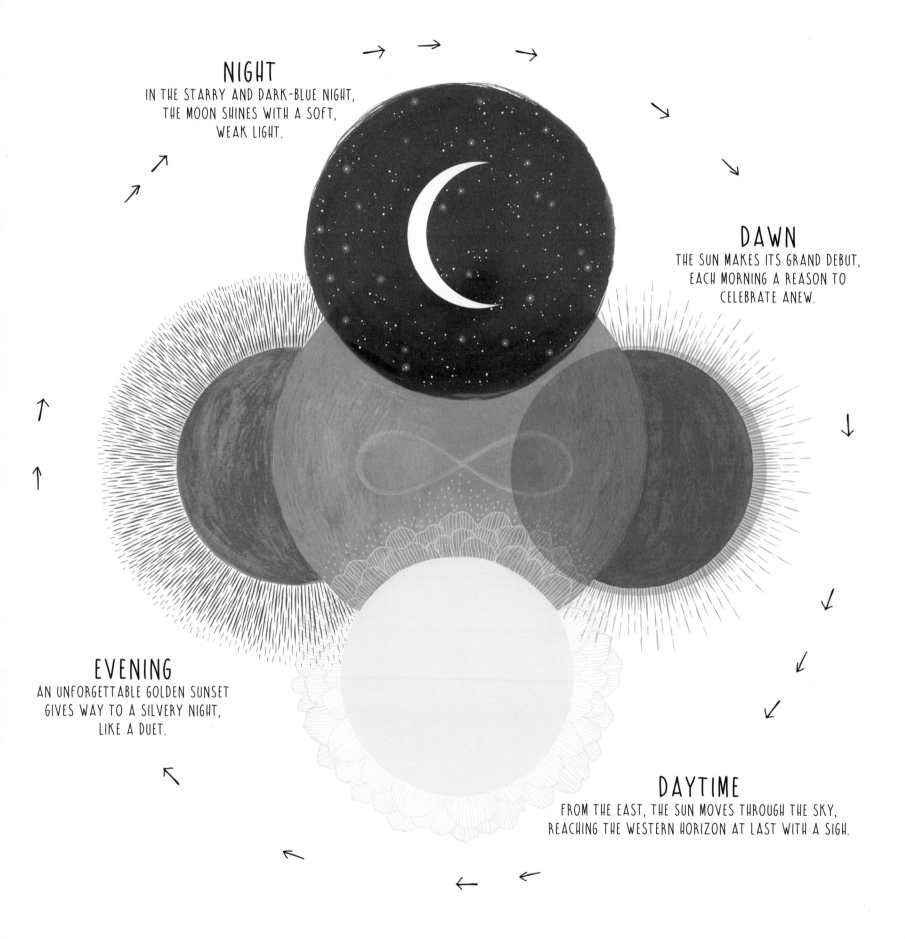

NIGHT
IN THE STARRY AND DARK-BLUE NIGHT, THE MOON SHINES WITH A SOFT, WEAK LIGHT.

DAWN
THE SUN MAKES ITS GRAND DEBUT, EACH MORNING A REASON TO CELEBRATE ANEW.

EVENING
AN UNFORGETTABLE GOLDEN SUNSET GIVES WAY TO A SILVERY NIGHT, LIKE A DUET.

DAYTIME
FROM THE EAST, THE SUN MOVES THROUGH THE SKY, REACHING THE WESTERN HORIZON AT LAST WITH A SIGH.

I WONDER WHETHER THE STARS
ARE SET ALIGHT IN HEAVEN SO THAT ONE DAY
EACH ONE OF US MAY FIND HIS OWN AGAIN.

— ANTOINE DE SAINT-EXUPÉRY
FRENCH WRITER AND AVIATOR

EVERY DAWN OFFERS US
THE CHANCE TO START OVER.
ISN'T THAT WONDERFUL?

THE LIFE CYCLE OF HUMAN BEINGS

IN THE BELLY OF A WOMAN
BEGINS THE MAGIC OF A NEW HUMAN.

GIVING BIRTH
FROM MOM'S TUMMY, NINE MONTHS AFTER,
A GIRL IS BORN AMID TEARS AND LAUGHTER.

A GIRL
SHE IS AN INFINITE
SOURCE OF ENERGY,
PLAYFULNESS, CURIOUSITY,
ADVENTURE, AND REVERIE.

PREGNANCY
WITH THE PROMISE OF
HER LOVE SO GREAT,
NEW LIFE GROWS INSIDE
AND LIES IN WAIT.

A WOMAN
SHE GROWS AND LEARNS EVERY DAY,
DANCING THROUGH LIFE LIKE A BALLET.

THE MOST FASCINATING IDEA IN THE WORLD
IS TO THINK ABOUT EVERYTHING THAT
HAD TO HAPPEN FOR YOU
TO BE HERE RIGHT NOW, READING THIS.
IT'S AN INCREDIBLE STORY
THAT HAS BEEN PASSED DOWN
FROM GENERATION TO GENERATION
TO OFFER US
THE MAGICAL OPPORTUNITY
TO ENJOY THIS UNIQUE
AND UNFORGETTABLE MOMENT.